WHO'S THE DADDY

A look at the most profitable sires to follow, both Flat and National Hunt, UK and Ireland and the best times to back their progeny.

Introduction.

If you already know...

Which sire has an incredible 20% strike rate on the Flat?

Which sire's four-year-olds have turned a profit of over 1000 points from just the 455 bets?

Which sire's all-weather two-year-olds have made over 300% profit?

Which successful Flat racer has made his followers a profit of over 700 points to level stakes – with his UK runners over HURDLES – and over 1300% profit if you limited your bets to his mares?

Which Derby-winning sire tops the Flat charts in Ireland with over 950% of profit with his fillies?

Which Flat winning son of Sadler's Wells has given us close to 400 winners in the UK over the last 10 years – over fences?

Which sire has provided a profit of over 900 points from just the 59 runners – when you back his five-year-olds in Irish bumpers?

... then you really should have written this book!

But if not, then you really need this information (and plenty more) to help to make your racing pay, and to take a different angle to your average losing punter.

Index

Why Listen To Me?

No-one wants to read about me, and I don't need to tell you my life story either, but a little background may at least let you know where I come from, what I know – and why the following pages may well prove well worth reading if you want to increase your chances of making a profit from the horses.

I have been involved in the sport for over 40 years now, starting on the local paper with a weekly article where I was paid the grand sum of a fiver, in the days when I had to write in block capitals with a pen and paper – and cycle to the offices to stick it through their letterbox every Sunday – and no, those weren't the good old days!

Since then I have been to college where I got a Distinction in Quantitative Studies (or Stats to you and I), and for the last 15 years or so I have been a full-time freelance racing journalist writing for all sorts – including The Independent, BetDaq, Alan Brazil Racing Club, What Really Wins, Australian Thoroughbred News, The Daily Sport, Press Association, Post Racing, Worldofsport, Timeform, and numerous others in a rich and varied career.

Like most (all?) punters, I have spent my lifetime searching for the Holy Grail – the system or the tipster who provides you with winner after winner, with all the associated dreams of wealth and happiness, but I have finally drawn the same conclusion that you should – it simply does not exist. If you are reading this thinking "Eureka" turn away now – the stats I have put together will not make you rich overnight – in fact they will undoubtedly find more losers than winners – but what they will do is narrow down the field to the likelier winners on any given racing day, if we assume past history can and does repeat itself – something nobody can ever guarantee – but what I can tell you is that this is my living – and if you stick rigidly to the rules suggested here and bet accordingly, putting in the necessary hard work to go with it – you won't go far wrong IN THE LONG TERM – overnight success belongs in fairy tales I am sorry to say.

What is this all about?

I have come to the conclusion that the only way to make regular profits from betting on horseracing is to go against the crowd. Frankel was the best horse in my lifetime (so far), and he retired unbeaten after 14 starts, but it was no secret just how good he was, and if you had backed him to £10 stakes on every run, all you would have made was £59.63 – or an average of £4.26 per bet. That takes nothing away from his brilliance, but everyone knew how good he was, and the only time he was any real value was on his debut – at odds of 7/4!

Ditto if you follow the top tipsters (including me) – so many people back their selections blindly that unless you are grabbing the value the moment their suggestions come out, the prices disappear in next to no time and you will struggle to make a profit – the bookies aren't fools and cut the prices as fast as they can as their liabilities add up.

So, as with all my other books (also available on Amazon by the way), I think we need to be thinking outside the box – finding a profitable angle that others miss and using it to our advantage.

This one is pretty simple once you get to grips with it – I have done most of the work in identifying the sires to follow and when – all you need to do (and I use the Racing Post website) is adjust the settings to show each horse's breeding – then look for the match ups before placing any bets.

Once again we are talking statistics – this will not be an interesting read but that was not the objective – we are looking for a profitable read so please be patient and the profits will be all yours.

One thing I do have to add – just like every walk of life things happen – some sires mentioned may be pensioned off, or taken out of "service"(pun intended) – or sadly passed away while I was researching this book – those details are close to impossible for me to track so apologies in advance if any sires mentioned fit that bracket – largely because they may still have runners to come.

NOTES

Data used is from 1st January 2013 to 17th April 2023.

All distances are recorded in furlongs – there are 8 furlongs to a mile (so 16 furlongs is two miles, 20 furlongs is two and a half miles etc).

A minimum of 100 qualifying runners were required to be included in any table

A filly becomes a mare when she reaches the age of four and above

Longest winning and losing runs were added for peace of mind and to assist with staking plans (if used) – my own preferred method is a 200 point bank to your own preferred stakes and then I bet 1pt per selection.

How To Make The Most Of This book.

Let me start with one sad but very simple fact – you will almost always make more money backing at Betfair SP than you will with the starting price from the bookmakers – fact. For that reason, ALL my profits and losses are declared to Betfair SP and NOT bookmaker SP as we are looking to make money, end of, and I have taken in to account the standard Betfair commission of 2% (correct at the time of writing) in all my figures.

The facts below speak for themselves – profits have been made on a regular basis by following these sires, and that will hopefully continue over the months and years ahead.

The Nitty Gritty

Those looking to profits by sires at various racecourses will be delighted to know that information already exists in my other books, so no need to repeat that here. To keep things neat and simple I will start by listing the top 5 most profitable to follow sires for the Flat (after all, money is the name of the game here) – as well as over hurdles, over fences, and in bumpers (covering all bases hopefully).

Each sire will then be analysed carefully by

Age of offspring
Going
Distance
Sex of offspring

Which will be notated by

Runners
Number of winners
Strike Rate
Profit
Longest winning run (LWR)
Longest losing run (LLR)

Using those figures you can then be as selective as you see fit – if you want an occasional bet, combine all the figures together and use those – if you want a bet most days, simply follow the sires concerned – the choice is yours.

So How Do I Find A Bet And Examples

Please be aware that as mentioned, this concept can have a long losing run BUT has proved to be very profitable in the long term – therefore I am taking the plunge and simply showing you how to find the horses for you to consider (whether you have a bet or not is down to you). Please excuse the small pictures – screen grabbing a race and keeping it all on one page means I have been forced to zoom out, but hopefully you will still get the idea.

Let's pick a single day (Tuesday 18th April 2023) as an example and see what comes out in the wash – I don't necessarily expect winners (this is a long-term thing as mentioned many times), but I can show you how to use this to find the right horses.

Firstly, go to www.racingpost.com.

RACING POST

Search horses, jockeys and trainers

Racecards   Results   News   Racing Tips   Raceday Live   Bloodstock   Sport Tips   Greyhounds   Shop

TODAY'S RACING

Going and non-runners >

LATEST   **TODAY**   TOMORROW   SATURDAY

Newmarket Flat I 7 races	**13:50** 9 Runners	**14:25** 9 Runners	**15:00** 13 Runners	**15:35** 7 Runners	**16:10** 7 Runners	**16:45** 7 Runners	**17:20** 10 Runners
Tipperary Jumps I 7 races	**14:05** 17 Runners	**14:40** 18 Runners	**15:15** 20 Runners	**15:50** 11 Runners	**16:25** 6 Runners	**17:00** 13 Runners	**17:35** 17 Runners
Lingfield (A.W) Flat I 7 races	**14:00** 7 Runners	**14:35** 7 Runners	**15:10** 6 Runners	**15:45** 8 Runners	**16:20** 7 Runners	**16:55** 8 Runners	**17:30** 8 Runners
Gowran Park Flat I 7 races	**16:03** 6 Runners	**16:38** 16 Runners	**17:13** 9 Runners	**17:45** 17 Runners	**18:15** 13 Runners	**18:45** 15 Runners	**19:15** 17 Runners
Southwell (A.W) Flat I 7 races	**17:25** 6 Runners	**18:00** 9 Runners	**18:30** 9 Runners	**19:00** 14 Runners	**19:30** 12 Runners	**20:00** 8 Runners	**20:30** 10 Runners
Newton Abbot Abandoned	14:15 Abandoned	14:50 Abandoned	15:23 Abandoned	15:58 Abandoned	16:33 Abandoned	17:08 Abandoned	

Then click on racecards (top left) and it will take you to this page

Racecards

Today's racecards, tips, form and betting for every racecourse in the UK and Ireland, and for the biggest racing fixtures in the international calendar.

Races   Runners Index   Stable Tours Entries

Then click on Newmarket to come to this page

Now we look, race by race. From now on I will only show races where we have a potential bet. The 1.50 isn't one, so we move on to the 2.25 – click on 2.25 and you come to this page.

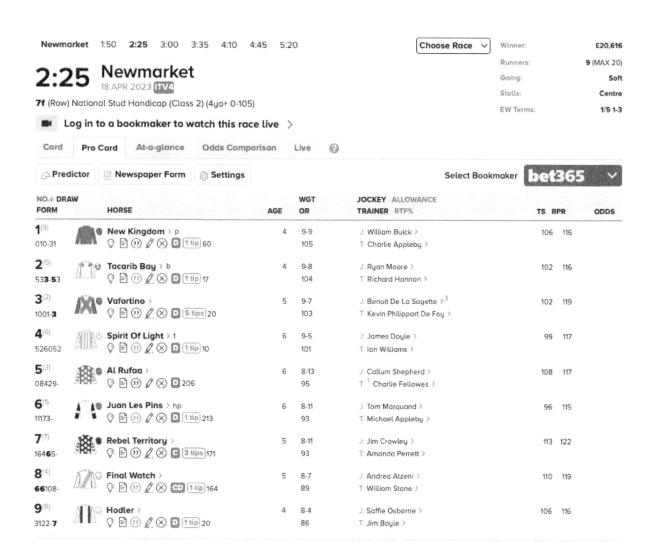

2:25 Newmarket
18 APR 2023 ITV4

7f (Row) National Stud Handicap (Class 2) (4yo+ 0-105)

			Winner:	£20,616
			Runners:	**9** (MAX 20)
Choose Race			Going:	Soft
			Stalls:	Centre
			EW Terms:	1/5 1-3

🎥 Log in to a bookmaker to watch this race live ›

Card | **Pro Card** | At-a-glance | Odds Comparison | Live | ❓

⛅ Predictor   📄 Newspaper Form   ⚙ Settings   Select Bookmaker **bet365** ⌄

NO.↓ DRAW FORM	HORSE	AGE	WGT OR	JOCKEY ALLOWANCE TRAINER RTF%	TS	RPR	ODDS
1(9) 010-31	New Kingdom › p	4	9-9 105	J: William Buick › T: Charlie Appleby ›	106	116	
2(5) 533-53	Tacarib Bay › b	4	9-8 104	J: Ryan Moore › T: Richard Hannon ›	102	116	
3(2) 1001-3	Vafortino ›	5	9-7 103	J: Benoit De La Sayette ›3 T: Kevin Philippart De Foy ›	102	119	
4(6) 526052	Spirit Of Light › t	6	9-5 101	J: James Doyle › T: Ian Williams ›	99	117	
5(3) 08429-	Al Rufaa ›	6	8-13 95	J: Callum Shepherd › T: Charlie Fellowes ›	108	117	
6(1) 11173-	Juan Les Pins › hp	6	8-11 93	J: Tom Marquand › T: Michael Appleby ›	96	115	
7(7) 16465-	Rebel Territory ›	5	8-11 93	J: Jim Crowley › T: Amanda Perrett ›	113	122	
8(4) 66108-	Final Watch ›	5	8-7 89	J: Andrea Atzeni › T: William Stone ›	110	119	
9(8) 3122-7	Hodler ›	4	8-4 86	J: Saffie Osborne › T: Jim Boyle ›	106	116	

But that doesn't easily show the info we need, so our next stop is to click on Settings (above the horses) to get here

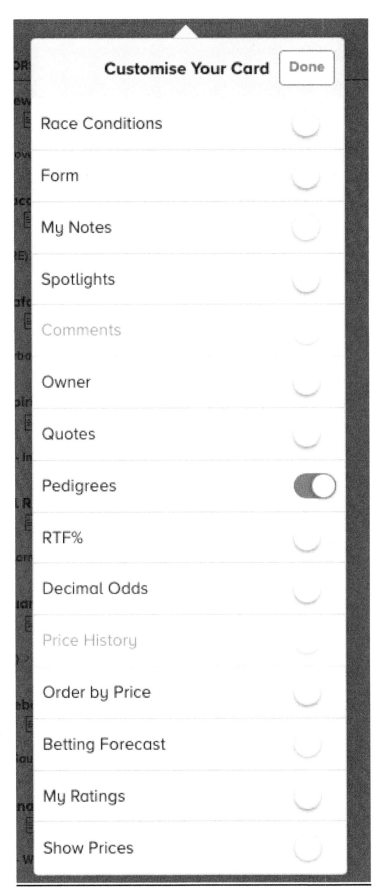

Customise Your Card Done

Race Conditions

Form

My Notes

Spotlights

Comments

Owner

Quotes

Pedigrees

RTF%

Decimal Odds

Price History

Order by Price

Betting Forecast

My Ratings

Show Prices

You can have as many or as few ticked as you want, but the one we NEED is as above - Pedigrees must be switched to "On" - this is available without subscription.

Click "Done" and the racecard will now look something like this

Newmarket   1:50   **2:25**   3:00   3:35   4:10   4:45   5:20   ~~Choose Race~~ ⌄

Winner:	£20,616
Runners:	9 (MAX 20)
Going:	Soft
Stalls:	Centre
EW Terms:	1/5 1-3

2:25 Newmarket
18 APR 2023 📺

7f (Row) National Stud Handicap (Class 2) (4yo+ 0-105)

📹 Log in to a bookmaker to watch this race live ›

Card   **Pro Card**   At-a-glance   Odds Comparison   Live   ⓘ

Predictor   📰 Newspaper Form   ⚙ Settings   Select Bookmaker **bet365** ⌄

NO. DRAW FORM	HORSE	AGE	WGT OR	JOCKEY ALLOWANCE TRAINER RTF%	TS	RPR	ODDS
1(9) 010-31	New Kingdom › p ♀📋⊚✎⊗ Ⓓ [1 tip] 60	4	9-9 105	J: William Buick › T: Charlie Appleby ›	106	116	
ch g Dubawi (IRE) › - Provenance (GB) › (Galileo (IRE)) ›							
2(5) 53**3-53**	Tacarib Bay › b ♀📋⊚✎⊗ Ⓓ [1 tip] 17	4	9-8 104	J: Ryan Moore › T: Richard Hannon ›	102	116	
b c Night Of Thunder (IRE) › - Bassmah (GB) › (Harbour Watch (IRE)) ›							
3(2) 1001-**3**	Vafortino › ♀📋⊚✎⊗ Ⓓ [5 tips] 20	5	9-7 103	J: Benoit De La Sayette ›3 T: Kevin Philippart De Foy ›	102	119	
b g New Bay (GB) › - Arbaah (USA) › (Invasor (ARG)) ›							
4(6) 526052	Spirit Of Light › ℄ ♀📋⊚✎⊗ Ⓓ [1 tip] 10	6	9-5 101	J: James Doyle › T: Ian Williams ›	99	117	
gr g Dark Angel (IRE) › - Inspiriter (GB) › (Invincible Spirit (IRE)) ›							
5(3) 08429-	Al Rufaa › ♀📋⊚✎⊗ Ⓓ 206	6	8-13 95	J: Callum Shepherd › T: Charlie Fellowes ›	108	117	
b g Kingman (GB) › - Clarmina (IRE) › (Cape Cross (IRE)) ›							
6(1) 11173-	Juan Les Pins › hp ♀📋⊚✎⊗ Ⓓ [1 tip] 213	6	8-11 93	J: Tom Marquand › T: Michael Appleby ›	96	115	
b g Invincible Spirit (IRE) › - Miss Cap Ferrat (GB) › (Darshaan (GB)) ›							
7(7) 164**6**5-	Rebel Territory › ♀📋⊚✎⊗ Ⓒ [3 tips] 171	5	8-11 93	J: Jim Crowley › T: Amanda Perrett ›	113	122	
b g Territories (IRE) › - Saucy Minx (IRE) › (Dylan Thomas (IRE)) ›							
8(4) **66**108-	Final Watch › ♀📋⊚✎⊗ ⒸⒹ [1 tip] 164	5	8-7 89	J: Andrea Atzeni › T: William Stone ›	110	119	
b g Mukhadram (GB) › - Watchoverme (GB) › (Haafhd (GB)) ›							
9(8) 3122-**7**	Hodler › ♀📋⊚✎⊗ Ⓓ [1 tip] 20	4	8-4 86	J: Saffie Osborne › T: Jim Boyle ›	106	116	
b g Sea The Moon (GER) › - Herzprinzessin (GER) › (Adlerflug (GER)) ›							

Now we have all that we need!

Looking through the race above we note:

The going is Soft (top right) – anything without "Standard" in the going description is on turf, so we now head to the UK Flat Turf chart below which gives us five sires – Sixties Icon, Bated Breath, Mount Nelson, Fountain of Youth, and Dubawi.

Each horse listed has his or her breeding underneath their name – the first horse, for example (New Kingdom) is described as

Ch g Dubawi (IRE) – Provenance (GB) (Galileo (IRE)

This translates as Chestnut Gelding by Dubawi (sire) out of Provenance (mare) who was sired by Galileo – all we need to note is that he is a gelding (if using the sex aspect of the horse) and Dubawi (one of our list of sires).

One look through the other horses shows us that NEW KINGDOM is the only horse who is a son or daughter of one of our Listed sires – he therefore becomes a potential bet.

Looking at Dubawi's other statistics we also note that his most profitable offspring are aged 3, their preferred going is Good To Firm, preferred distance is 10 furlongs, and preferred sex is a filly. Here we have a different age, different going (soft) different distance (seven furlongs) and different sex (gelding), so personally my bet size (if any) would be reduced considerably, but it's your money and your choice!

RESULT 2.25pm NEWMARKET

NEW KINGDOM 8th 4/1 (6.08 BSP)

Don't panic, I won't be going into that kind of detail again (you have the main race to fall back on) but looking though all the other cards on the day I found the following races to consider:

2.00pm Lingfield (All-Weather)

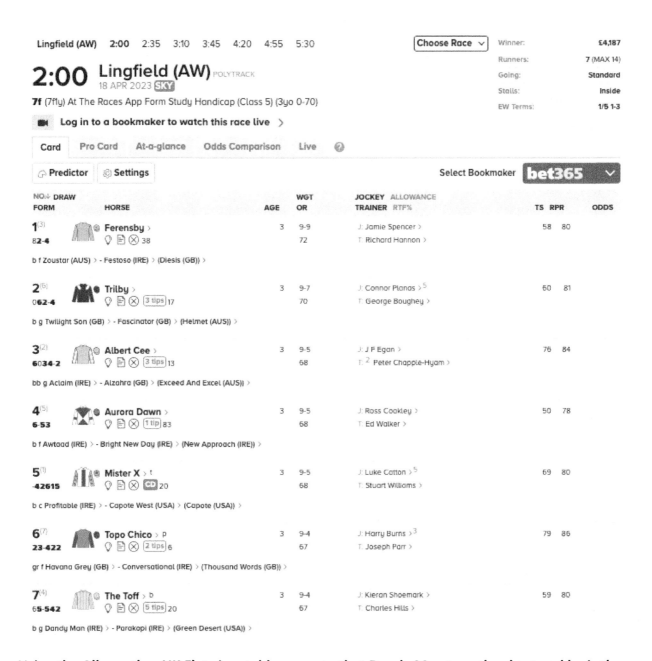

2:00 Lingfield (AW) POLYTRACK
18 APR 2023 SKY

7f (7fly) At The Races App Form Study Handicap (Class 5) (3yo 0-70)

					Winner:	£4,187
					Runners:	7 (MAX 14)
					Going:	Standard
					Stalls:	Inside
					EW Terms:	1/5 1-3

Choose Race ⌄

📹 Log in to a bookmaker to watch this race live   ›

Card   Pro Card   At-a-glance   Odds Comparison   Live   ❔

⌂ Predictor   ⚙ Settings   Select Bookmaker **bet365** ⌄

NO. DRAW FORM	HORSE	AGE	WGT OR	JOCKEY ALLOWANCE TRAINER RTF%	TS	RPR	ODDS
1 (3) 82-4	Ferensby ›	3	9-9 72	J: Jamie Spencer › T: Richard Hannon ›	58	80	
b f Zoustar (AUS) › - Festoso (IRE) › (Diesis (GB)) ›							
2 (6) 062-4	Trilby › ♀ 📄 ⊗ [3 tips] 17	3	9-7 70	J: Connor Planas › 5 T: George Boughey ›	60	81	
b g Twilight Son (GB) › - Fascinator (GB) › (Helmet (AUS)) ›							
3 (2) 6034-2	Albert Cee › ♀ 📄 ⊗ [3 tips] 13	3	9-5 68	J: J F Egan › T: 2 Peter Chapple-Hyam ›	76	84	
bb g Aclaim (IRE) › - Alzahra (GB) › (Exceed And Excel (AUS)) ›							
4 (5) 6-53	Aurora Dawn › ♀ 📄 ⊗ [1 tip] 83	3	9-5 68	J: Ross Coakley › T: Ed Walker ›	50	78	
b f Awtaad (IRE) › - Bright New Day (IRE) › (New Approach (IRE)) ›							
5 (1) -42615	Mister X › t ♀ 📄 ⊗ CD 20	3	9-5 68	J: Luke Catton › 5 T: Stuart Williams ›	69	80	
b c Profitable (IRE) › - Capote West (USA) › (Capote (USA)) ›							
6 (7) 23-422	Topo Chico › P ♀ 📄 ⊗ [2 tips] 6	3	9-4 67	J: Harry Burns › 3 T: Joseph Parr ›	79	86	
gr f Havana Grey (GB) › - Conversational (IRE) › (Thousand Words (GB)) ›							
7 (4) 65-542	The Toff › b ♀ 📄 ⊗ [5 tips] 20	3	9-4 67	J: Kieran Shoemark › T: Charles Hills ›	59	80	
b g Dandy Man (IRE) › - Parakopi (IRE) › (Green Desert (USA)) ›							

Using the All-weather UK Flat sires table we note that Dandy Man tops the chart and he is the sire of horse 7, The Toff. Looking at more detail about the sire we also note that his most profitable lines are two-years olds, running over five furlongs, and geldings. The Toff is a three-year-old, this race is over seven furlongs, but Yes, he is a gelding. Again, for me personally, not all the boxes are ticked, but they rarely are so I would still have a small bet.

RESULT 2.00pm LINGFIELD

THE TOFF WON 100/30 (BSP 6.0)

3.10pm Lingfield (All Weather)

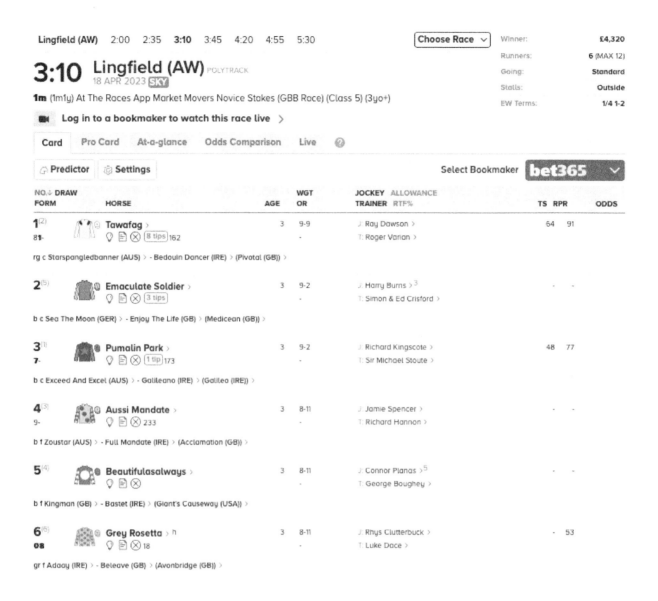

In this case the runner we are talking about is Pumalin Park, a son of Exceed And Excel who sits at number 4 in the all-weather list. Again, his profitable stats are two-year-olds, a mile, and geldings. This horse is a three-year-old colt but he is running over a mile so he becomes worthy of consideration.

RESULT 3.10pm LINGFIELD

PUMALIN PARK WON 7/4 (BSP 2.96)

3.45pm Lingfield (All-Weather)

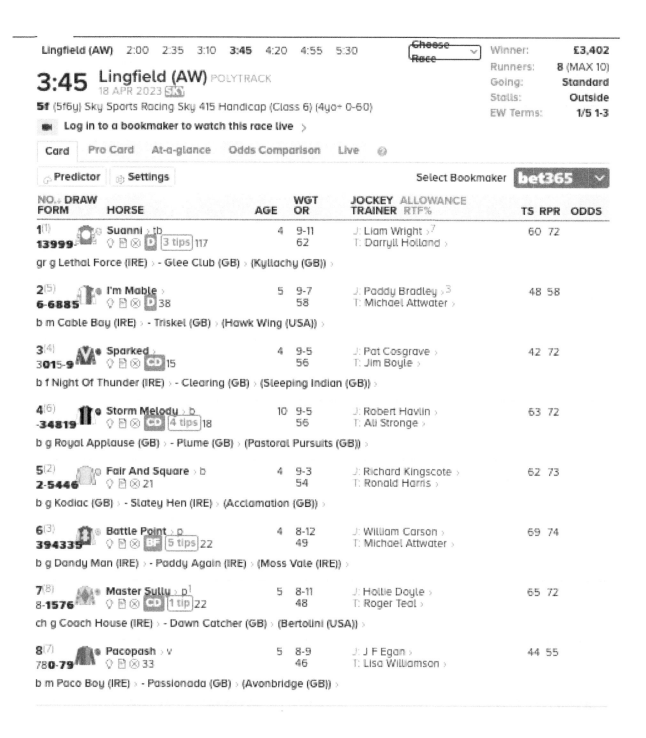

Once again it's our old mate Dandy Man, the father of horse number 6 Battle Point. This race is over five furlongs, and the horse is a four-year-old gelding. Trip and gelding status are boxes ticked so another to consider on the day.

RESULT 3.45pm LINGFIELD

BATTLE POINT WON 5/1 (BSP 6.26)

6.00pm Southwell

Southwell (AW) 5:25 **6:00** 6:30 7:00 7:30 8:00 8:30

Choose Race

Winner:	£3,402
Runners:	9 (MAX 14)
Going:	Standard
Stalls:	Inside
EW Terms:	1/5 1-3

6:00 Southwell (AW) TAPETA
18 APR 2023 SKY

1m3f (1m3f23y) Cazoo Handicap (Class 6) (4yo+ 0-60)

📷 Log in to a bookmaker to watch this race live >

Card | Pro Card | At-a-glance | Odds Comparison | Live | ⓘ

Predictor | Settings   Select Bookmaker **bet365** ⌄

NO. DRAW FORM	HORSE	AGE	WGT OR	JOCKEY ALLOWANCE TRAINER RTF%	TS	RPR	ODDS
1(5) 78-875	Bay Of Naples > ♀ 📋 ⊗ **C D** 14	7	9-10 61	J: Tom Eaves > T: Michael Herrington >	48	71	
b g Exceed And Excel (AUS) > - Copperbeech (IRE) > (Red Ransom (USA)) >							
2(6) 31131-	Silver Bubble > ♀ 📋 ⊗ 3 tips 196	5	9-10 61	J: Ben Curtis > T: Gay Kelleway >	-	73	
gr m Mayson (GB) > - Skyrider (IRE) > (Dalakhani (IRE)) >							
3(9) 577	Stan > h ♀ 📋 ⊗ 1 tip 13	4	9-9 60	J: Trevor Whelan > T: Kevin Frost >	55	69	
b g Highland Reel (IRE) > - Scottish Stage (IRE) > (Selkirk (USA)) >							
4(4) 503-94	Tio Mio > t ♀ 📋 ⊗ 21	5	9-7 58	J: Gina Mangan >5 T: Gary Hanmer >	41	71	
b g Teofilo (IRE) > - Celeste De La Mer (IRE) > (Zoffany (IRE)) >							
5(1) 2257-8	Make A Prophet > ♀ 📋 ⊗ 46	4	9-3 54	J: Paul Mulrennan > T: Paul Midgley >	51	66	
b g Divine Prophet (AUS) > - Miss Mirabeau (GB) > (Oasis Dream (GB)) >							
6(8) 7-7422	Amourie > p ♀ 📋 ⊗ **C** 4 tips 5	7	9-3 54	J: Mark Winn >5 T: Ray Craggs >	64	74	
ch m Haafhd (GB) > - Tour D'Amour (IRE) > (Fruits Of Love (USA)) >							
7(7) 721942	Destinado > ♀ 📋 ⊗ 5 tips 12	5	9-0 51	J: Mollie Phillips >3 T: Tony Carroll >	56	72	
b g Lope De Vega (IRE) > - Contribution (GB) > (Champs Elysees (GB)) >							
8(2) 25-300	Tom Hazelgrove > t¹ ♀ 📋 ⊗ 67	4	8-9 46	J: Josephine Gordon > T: Phil McEntee >	43	64	
gr g Alhebayeb (IRE) > - With A Twist (GB) > (Excellent Art (GB)) >							
9(3) 8080-7	Mad Artymaise > w² ♀ 📋 ⊗ 14	4	8-9 46	J: Aiden Brookes >5 T: Gillian Boanas >	52	65	
ch f Dandy Man (IRE) > - El Mirage (IRE) > (Elusive Quality (USA)) >							

For the first time we have a race with not one but TWO qualifiers – Bay Of Naples (Exceed and Excel) and Mad Artymaise (Dandy Man) – this time I will leave it to you to look at the chart per sire and draw your own conclusions!

RESULT 6.00pm SOUTHWELL

BAY OF NAPLES 2ND 4/1 (BSP 5.4), MAD ARTYMAISE 4TH 50/1 (BSP 80.0)

7.30pm Southwell

		Winner:	**£3,402**
		Runners:	**12** (MAX 14)

7:30 Southwell (AW) TAPETA
18 APR 2023 SKY

		Going:	**Standard**
		Stalls:	**Inside**
		EW Terms:	**1/5 1-4**

7f (7f14y) Jigsaw Sports Branding Handicap (Class 6) (4yo+ 0-60)

Log in to a bookmaker to watch this race live ›

Card   Pro Card   At-a-glance   Odds Comparison   Live   @

Predictor   Settings   Select Bookmaker **bet365** ∨

NO. DRAW FORM	HORSE	AGE	WGT OR	JOCKEY ALLOWANCE TRAINER RTF%	TS	RPR	ODDS
1(11) 585328	Tathmeen › p ♀ 🖪 ⊗ C 5	8	9-11 62	J: Cam Hardie › T: Antony Brittain ›	59	71	
	b g Exceed And Excel (AUS) › - Deyaar (USA) › (Storm Cat (USA)) ›						
2(7) 0990-7	Mudlahhim › ♀ 🖪 ⊗ D 36	7	9-10 61	J: Elisha Whittington › 5 T: Scott Dixon ›	62	72	
	b g Tamayuz (GB) › - So Sweet (IRE) › (Cape Cross (IRE)) ›						
3(2) 57-625	Mashaan › t ♀ 🖪 ⊗ D 3 tips 24	5	9-9 60	J: Clifford Lee › T: Shaun Lycett ›	64	75	
	b g Kodiac (GB) › - Vitello (GB) › (Raven's Pass (USA)) ›						
4(3) /3508-	Depart A Minuit › ♀ 🖪 ⊗ 305	4	9-8 59	J: Dylan Hogan › T: 1 Stella Barclay ›	-	66	
	b g1 Twilight Son (GB) › - Grand Depart (GB) › (Royal Applause (GB)) ›						
5(8) 98537-	Swinging Eddie › ♀ 🖪 ⊗ D 186	7	9-8 59	J: Oliver Stammers › 3 T: Grant Tuer ›	39	69	
	b g Swiss Spirit (GB) › - Bling Bling (IRE) › (Indian Ridge (IRE)) ›						
6(12) 252133	Written Broadcast › b ♀ 🖪 ⊗ CD 3 tips 9	6	9-7 58	J: Mark Winn › 5 T: Ollie Pears ›	65	74	
	gr g Gutaifan (IRE) › - Teeline (IRE) › (Exceed And Excel (AUS)) ›						
7(4) 1824-1	Northbound › ♀ 🖪 ⊗ CD 6 tips 14	5	9-7 58	J: Paul Hanagan › T: Julie Camacho ›	50	76	
	b g Fast Company (IRE) › - Natalisa (IRE) › (Green Desert (USA)) ›						
8(10) 23094	Key Look › ♀ 🖪 ⊗ D 130	6	9-7 58	J: Graham Lee › T: 1 Paul Midgley ›	42	74	
	ch m Dawn Approach (IRE) › - Fashion Line (IRE) › (Cape Cross (IRE)) ›						
9(6) 20-916	Turbo Command › ♀ 🖪 ⊗ CD 33	6	9-6 57	J: Paul Mulrennan › T: Alison Hamilton ›	54	72	
	gr g War Command (USA) › - The Tempest (GB) › (Mastercraftsman (IRE)) ›						
10(5) 10150-	Amelia R › ♀ 🖪 ⊗ D 176	7	9-3 54	J: Zak Wheatley › 5 T: Ray Craggs ›	-	73	
	b m Zoffany (IRE) › - Xaloc (IRE) › (Shirocco (GER)) ›						
11(1) 07-390	Willing To Please › ♀ 🖪 ⊗ D 18	6	9-0 51	J: Ben Curtis › T: Philip Kirby ›	59	70	
	b m Iffraaj (GB) › - Tebee's Oasis (GB) › (Oasis Dream (GB)) ›						
12(9) 00-618	Boarhunt › ♀ 🖪 ⊗ D 33	4	8-11 48	J: Luke Morris › T: Michael Appleby ›	49	73	
	b g Equiano (FR) › - Guishan (GB) › (Ishiguru (USA)) ›						

Ho

rse number One, Tathmeen is a son of Exceed And Excel

RESULT 7.30pm SOUTHWELL

THATHMEEN 4TH 12/1 (BSP 20.94)

8.30pm Southwell

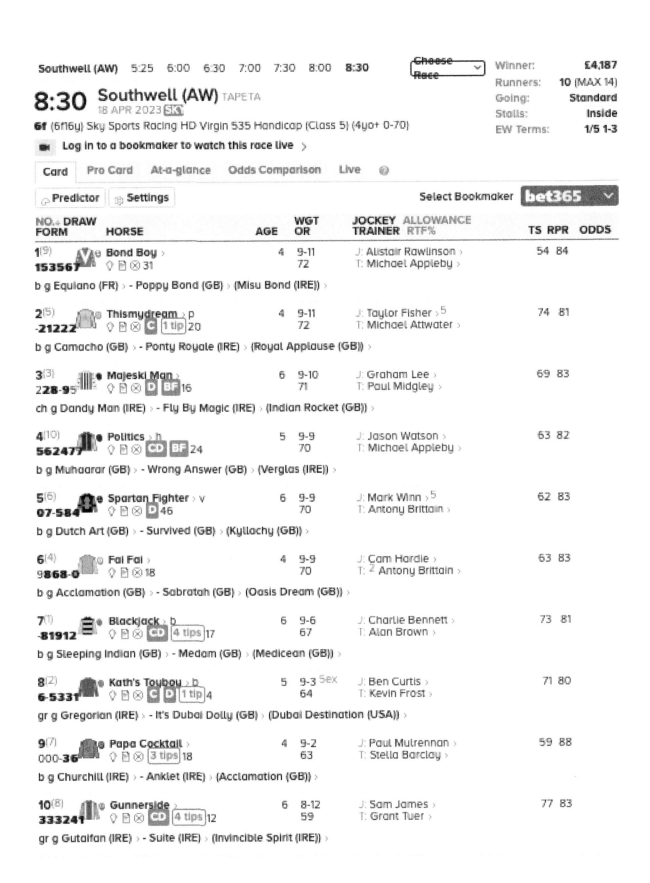

Our old mate Dandy Man is back, this time with Horse Number 3, Majeski Man

RESULT 8.30pm SOUTHWELL

MAJESKI MAN 7TH 11/1 (BSP 16.34)

3.50pm Tipperary

Choose Race ▼

Winner:	€6,490
Runners:	11
Going:	Yielding
No. of fences:	
EW Terms:	1/5 1-3

3:50 Tipperary
18 APR 2023 [RTE]
2m1½f (2m1f105y) Ballykisteen Beginners Chase (5yo+)

🔴 Place a bet through the Racing Post to watch live

Card   Pro Card   At-a-glance   Odds Comparison   Live   @

⊙ Predictor   ⚙ Settings   Select Bookmaker **bet365** ⌄

NO. FORM	HORSE	AGE	WGT OR	JOCKEY TRAINER	ALLOWANCE RTF%	TS	RPR	ODDS
1 /57-09	**Brawler** › tp ♀ 🗎 ⊗ 120	8	11-12 112	J: Denis O'Regan › T: Patrick T Foley ›		-	123	
b g Teofilo (IRE) › - Red Avis (GB) › (Exceed And Excel (AUS)) ›								
2 -54445	**Changing The Rules** › ♀ 🗎 ⊗ 1 tip 9	6	11-12 -	J: Jody McGarvey › T: Mrs John Harrington ›		55	127	
b g Walk In The Park (IRE) › - Blooming Quick (IRE) › (Moscow Society (USA)) ›								
3 B-P1P2	**Clifton Warrior** › ♀ 🗎 ⊗ BF 2 tips 37	7	11-12 -	J: Rachael Blackmore › T: Henry De Bromhead ›		47	130	
ch g Schiaparelli (GER) › - Alina Rheinberg (GER) › (Waky Nao (GB)) ›								
4 4-5565	**Flindt** › tp¹ ♀ 🗎 ⊗ D 37	8	11-12 112	J: Simon Torrens › T: Ciaran Murphy ›		63	100	
b g Most Improved (IRE) › - Aries Ballerina (IRE) › (Peintre Celebre (USA)) ›								
5 0-**P53**7	**General Dynamics** › ht ♀ 🗎 ⊗ 32	7	11-12 -	J: Miss A McGuinness ›[7] T: J J Lambe ›		34	64	
b g Califet (FR) › - Histoire De Moeurs (FR) › (Kaldounevees (FR)) ›								
6 **1**141F/	**Heather Rocco** › ♀ 🗎 ⊗ BF 720	8	11-12 -	J: Darragh O'Keeffe › T: Henry De Bromhead ›		-	-	
ch g Shirocco (GER) › - Liss A Chara (IRE) › (Presenting (GB)) ›								
7 -22F34	**Mattie's Mountain** › tp ♀ 🗎 ⊗ 23	8	11-12 118	J: Phillip Enright › T: Eoin Christopher McCarthy ›		93	117	
b g Mountain High (IRE) › - Ballyeightra Lass (IRE) › (Witness Box (USA)) ›								
9 8347UF	**The Banger Doyle** › ♀ 🗎 ⊗ 1 tip 38	7	11-12 -	J: Ian Power › T: John Queally ›		-	136	
ch g Windsor Knot (IRE) › - Knockcroghery (IRE) › (Pelder (IRE)) ›								
10 103285	**Diamondinthemud** › ♀ 🗎 ⊗ 31	7	11-5 -	J: Sean Flanagan › T: Nigel Thomas Slevin ›		49	119	
b m Getaway (GER) › - Good Looking Woman (IRE) › (Oscar (IRE)) ›								
11 979170	**Premier Queen** › ♀ 🗎 ⊗ D 29	7	11-5 -	J: Kieren Buckley ›[3] T: Mrs Prunella Dobbs ›		-	-	
ch m Presenting (GB) › - Premier Victory (IRE) › (Winged Love (IRE)) ›								
12 66-3P3	**Red As Rust** › ♀ 🗎 ⊗ 31	10	11-5 118	J: Conor Orr › T: Nigel Thomas Slevin ›		91	129	
ch m Shantou (USA) › - Milbig Lass (IRE) › (Shernazar (GB)) ›								

Our first National Hunt suggestion of the day when horse number 9, The Banger Doyle goes over fences here as a son of Windsor Knot.

RESULT 3.50pm TIPPERARY

THE BANGER DOYLE WON 13/2 (BSP 10.23)

4.25pm Tipperary

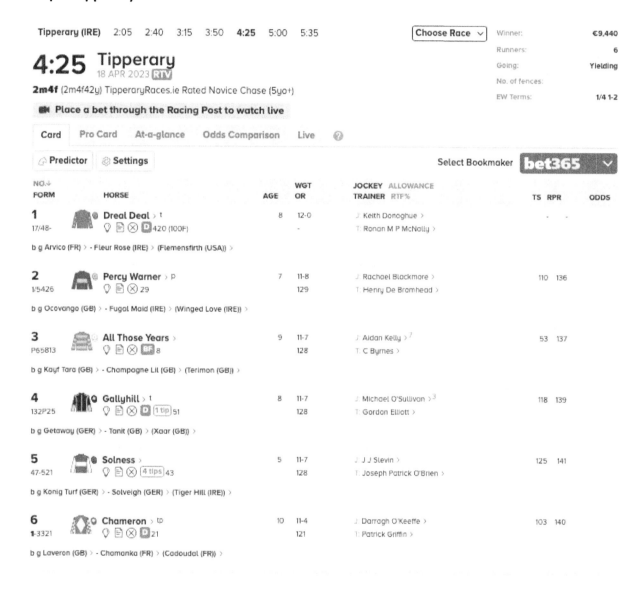

Here we go again, this time horse number 3, All Those Years, is a son of Kayf Tara

RESULT 4.25pm TIPPERARY

ALL THOSE YEARS FELL 5/2 (BSP 4.49
5.00pm Tipperary

2m7½f (2m7f135y) Tipperary Handicap Chase (5yo+ 0-109)

	Runners:	12
	Going:	Yielding
	No. of fences:	
	EW Terms:	1/5 1-4

🔴 Place a bet through the Racing Post to watch live

Card	Pro Card	At-a-glance	Odds Comparison	Live	ⓘ

Predictor	Settings		Select Bookmaker	bet365 ⌄

NO.↓ FORM	HORSE	AGE	WGT OR	JOCKEY ALLOWANCE TRAINER RTF%	TS	RPR	ODDS
1 61381P	Secret Cargo › ♀ 🗎 ⊗ 197	9	12-0 107	J: Niall Moore ›7 T: Philip Fenton ›	76	114	
2 8U5024	Goodnightgodbless › p ♀ 🗎 ⊗ C D BF 2 tips 54	10	11-7 100	J: Aidan Kelly ›7 T: J Motherway ›	78	117	
3 P3425U	Earths Furies › b¹ ♀ 🗎 ⊗ D 12	7	11-6 99	J: Miss M O'Sullivan ›5 T: Eugene M O'Sullivan ›	39	105	
4 B32232	Positive Thinker › ♀ 🗎 ⊗ BF 1 tip 19	6	11-6 99	J: Sean O'Keeffe › T: Michael J McDonagh ›	-	-	
5 -53523	Baldur's Gate › ♀ 🗎 ⊗ 1 tip 18	8	11-5 98	J: Rachael Blackmore › T: Miss Denise Marie O'Shea ›	91	111	
7 -90P86	Mansoline › t ♀ 🗎 ⊗ 9	7	10-13 92	J: Phillip Enright › T: Brian M McMahon ›	37	110	
8 262233	Mahler Appeal › p ♀ 🗎 ⊗ 18	7	10-10 89	J: Michael O'Sullivan ›3 T: Garrett James Power ›	40	104	
9 -71F80	Bearwithmenow › ♀ 🗎 ⊗ D 171	6	10-8 87	J: Darragh O'Keeffe › T: J P Flavin ›	-	-	
10 -66530	Da Big Fella › p ♀ 🗎 ⊗ 68	9	10-3 82	J: J J Slevin › T: Eamon Courtney ›	-	108	
11 728512	Eddies Pride › ht ♀ 🗎 ⊗ D 12	9	10-3 82	J: G B Noonan ›5 T: Norman Lee ›	75	112	
12 P9P1PP	Four Country Roads › ♀ 🗎 ⊗ D 18	9	10-0 79	J: Diarmuid Moloney ›7 T: Brian M McMahon ›	58	108	
13 5-16PP	Larkfield Legacy › ♀ 🗎 ⊗ 18	9	10-0 79	J: Simon Torrens › T: R P Rath ›	53	116	
NR 4P2P1P	Aodhan May › ♀ 🗎 ⊗ 1	7	10-13 92	J: T: C Burnes ›	83	113	

b g Mahler (GB) › - Duffys Hall (IRE) › (Saddlers' Hall (IRE)) ›

b m Yeats (IRE) › - La Sarrazine (FR) › (Medicean (GB)) ›

b g Dylan Thomas (IRE) › - Verney Roe (IRE) › (Vinnie Roe (IRE)) ›

b g Ocovango (GB) › - Clip Her Tail (IRE) › (Old Vic (GB)) ›

b g Stowaway (GB) › - Like A Miller (IRE) › (Luso (GB)) ›

ch m Brave Mansonnien (FR) › - Line Mai (FR) › (Sleeping Car (FR)) ›

ch g Mahler (GB) › - Murphys Appeal (IRE) › (Lord Of Appeal (GB)) ›

bb g Notnowcato (GB) › - Dante Anna (IRE) › (Anshan (GB)) ›

b g Gold Well (GB) › - Shuil Dara (IRE) › (Presenting (GB)) ›

b m Flemensfirth (USA) › - Coscorrig (IRE) › (Pistolet Bleu (IRE)) ›

br g Arcadio (GER) › - Sunny South East (IRE) › (Gothland (FR)) ›

b m Kalanisi (IRE) › - Larkfield Lady (IRE) › (Heron Island (IRE)) ›

Horse number 2, Goodnightgodbless is a daughter of Yeats

RESULT 5.00pm TIPPERARY

GOODNIGHTGODBLESS 5TH 7/1 (BSP 10.0)

5.35pm Tipperary

5:35 Tipperary
18 APR 2023 RTV

Winner:	€6,490
Runners:	17
Going:	Yielding
EW Terms:	1/5 1-3

2m4f (2m4145y) Irish Stallion Farms EBF Mares INH Flat Race (5yo+)

🎥 Place a bet through the Racing Post to watch live

Card   Pro Card   At-a-glance   Odds Comparison   Live   ⓘ

⟳ Predictor   ⚙ Settings

Select Bookmaker   **bet365** ⌄

NO.↑ FORM	HORSE	AGE	WGT OR	JOCKEY TRAINER ALLOWANCE RTF%	TS RPR ODDS
1 32	Armed And Fabulous › ♀ 📄 ⊗ 26	5	11-11 -	J: Mr T Hamilton › T: Ms Margaret Mullins ›	52 97
2	Danpet › ♀ 📄 ⊗	6	11-11 -	J: Mr H C Swan ›5 T: Patrick T Foley ›	- -
3	Four Clean Aces › ♀ 📄 ⊗ 2 tips	5	11-11 -	J: Mr P W Mullins › T: W P Mullins ›	- -
4 65-5	Getaway Rua › ♀ 📄 ⊗ 26	7	11-11 -	J: Mr Pat Taaffe ›7 T: John Queally ›	22 76
5 944	Hob's Angel › ♀ 📄 ⊗ 278	7	11-11 -	J: Mr J W Hendrick ›7 T: Martin Gerard McGuane ›	61 89
6 607	Holly Tree › ♀ 📄 ⊗ 26	6	11-11 -	J: Mr P A King ›5 T: William P Murphy ›	29 103
7 4P3	Impulse › ♀ 📄 ⊗ 2 tips 19	5	11-11 -	J: Mr Finian Maguire › T: ²Liam G O'Brien ›	- 104
8	Joya Del Mar › ♀ 📄 ⊗	5	11-11 -	J: Mr D McGill ›7 T: Dermot A McLoughlin ›	- -
9	Koko Kan › ♀ 📄 ⊗	5	11-11 -	J: Mr J L Gleeson ›7 T: Peter Fahey ›	- -
10	Magic Olinger › ♀ 📄 ⊗	5	11-11 -	J: Mr J Dunne ›7 T: Gerard Keane ›	- -
11 9-564	Matilda Park › ♀ 📄 ⊗ 54	5	11-11 -	J: Miss J Townend › T: G Ahern ›	30 103
12 154	Mousey Brown › t ♀ 📄 ⊗ 37	6	11-11 -	J: Mr J C Barry ›3 T: ²Dermot A McLoughlin ›	41 84

b m Affinisea (IRE) › - Reconbustible (IRE) › (Mr Combustible (IRE)) ›

ch m Soldier Of Fortune (IRE) › - Tessoli (IRE) › (King's Theatre (IRE)) ›

b m Saint Des Saints (FR) › - Queen Alphabet (IRE) › (King's Theatre (IRE)) ›

ch m Getaway (GER) › - Utrillo's Art (IRE) › (Medecis (GB)) ›

b m Mahler (GB) › - Kiss Debride (IRE) › (Oscar (IRE)) ›

b m Arcadio (GER) › - Lisdaleen (IRE) › (Saddlers' Hall (IRE)) ›

bb m Free Port Lux (GB) › - Venus De Beaumont (FR) › (Assessor (IRE)) ›

b m Ol' Man River (IRE) › - Sand Reef (IRE) › (Footstepsinthesand (GB)) ›

ch m Soldier Of Fortune (IRE) › - Deep Supreme (IRE) › (Supreme Leader (GB)) ›

b m Imperial Monarch (IRE) › - Giftcraft (IRE) › (Presenting (GB)) ›

b m Milan (GB) › - Deep Lilly (GB) › (Glacial Storm (USA)) ›

b m Califet (FR) › - Desperado Queen (IRE) › (Un Desperado (FR)) ›

| 13 | Penelope's Charm ⚥ 🗎 ⊗ | 5 | 11-11 - | J: Mr E P O'Brien ›5 T: Daniel William O'Sullivan › | - - |

b m Make Believe (GB) › - Penelope Star (GER) › (Acatenango (GER)) ›

| 14 | Starry Heights ⚥ 🗎 ⊗ 19 | 5 | 11-11 - | J: Mr T Power Roche ›7 T: N Dooly › | 50 86 |
| 076 | | | | | |

b m Hillstar (GB) › - Call Her Something (IRE) › (Heron Island (IRE)) ›

| 15 | Tin Of Tonic ⚥ 🗎 ⊗ | 5 | 11-11 - | J: Miss M O'Sullivan ›5 T: Eugene M O'Sullivan › | - - |

b m Soldier Of Fortune (IRE) › - Janebailey (GB) › (Silver Patriarch (IRE)) ›

| 16 | Vedetta Star ⚥ 🗎 ⊗ 59 | 5 | 11-11 - | J: Mr D G Lavery › T: Peter Fahey › | 27 92 |
| 4 | | | | | |

ch m Flemensfirth (USA) › - Princess Gaia (IRE) › (King's Theatre (IRE)) ›

| 17 | World Of Fortunes ⚥ 🗎 ⊗ | 5 | 11-11 - | J: Mr L J Murphy ›7 T: Liam Kenny › | - - |

ch m Soldier Of Fortune (IRE) › - Rose Of The World (IRE) › (Vinnie Roe (IRE)) ›

A huge field here sees two qualifiers in Number 5 Hob's Angel (a daughter of Mahler) and number 12 Mousey Brown (a daughter of Califet).

RESULT 5.35pm TIPPERARY

HOB'S ANGEL 10TH 50/1 (BSP 67.1) MOUSEY BROWN 5TH 66/1 (BSP 110.54)

5.45pm Gowran Park

5:45 Gowran Park
18 APR 2023 RTV

1m1½f (1m1f130y) Thanks To All Our Sponsors Handicap (4yo+ 47-65)

		Winner:	€6,195
		Runners:	17
		Going:	Soft
		Stalls:	
		EW Terms:	1/5 1-5

🔴 Place a bet through the Racing Post to watch live

| Card | Pro Card | At-a-glance | Odds Comparison | Live | ⓘ |

| ⊙ Predictor | ⚙ Settings | | Select Bookmaker | bet365 ⌄ |

NO. DRAW FORM	HORSE	AGE	WGT OR	JOCKEY ALLOWANCE TRAINER RTF%	TS	RPR	ODDS
1(4) -75738	Emperor Of Silk › ♀ 🖹 ⊗ 33	6	10-2 65	J: Jack Cleary ›7 T: Anthony Mullins ›	-	76	
2(13) 36683-	King Of The Kippax › ♀ 🖹 ⊗ 194	4	9-11 60	J: Mark Enright › T: 1 Leanne Breen ›	59	69	
3(10) 0P-936	Jazz Dreamers › ♀ 🖹 ⊗ 33	5	9-9 58	J: Oisin McSweeney ›5 T: Seamus Fahey ›	49	77	
4(2) 79335	Shona Mea › v ♀ 🖹 ⊗ CD 1 tip 130	6	9-8 57	J: Scott McCullagh ›3 T: Mrs John Harrington ›	60	78	
5(8) 39049-	Contrapposto › ♀ 🖹 ⊗ 123 (113J)	9	9-7 56	J: Ben Coen › T: R Donohoe ›	42	77	
6(19) 8950-0	Lofoten › ♀ 🖹 ⊗ 24	5	9-7 56	J: Colin Keane › T: P J Rothwell ›	43	69	
7(17) 1/033-	Astrophysicist › tb ♀ 🖹 ⊗ CD 1 tip 169 (26J)	5	9-5 54	J: W J Lee › T: J A Nash ›	54	74	
8(12) 5/0/1/	Bigz Belief › tb ♀ 🖹 ⊗ 724 (29J)	6	9-5 54	J: Declan McDonogh › T: Matthew J Smith ›	-	66	
9(14) 59-271	Chimeric › p ♀ 🖹 ⊗ 57	6	9-4 53	J: Donagh O'Connor › T: J F Levins ›	50	70	
10(18) 00079-	Griseo › ♀ 🖹 ⊗ 270	4	9-3 52	J: Robbie Colgan › T: 1 V C Ward ›	36	69	
11(1) 69009-	Zaghraf › ♀ 🖹 ⊗ BF 280 (19J)	4	9-3 52	J: J M Sheridan ›3 T: Denis Gerard Hogan ›	62	74	
12(6) 1744-4	Dragon Roll › ♀ 🖹 ⊗ C 102	7	9-0 49	J: Seamie Heffernan › T: Eamonn O'Connell ›	51	71	

b g Holy Roman Emperor (IRE) › - Silk Dress (IRE) › (Gulch (USA)) ›

b g Almanzor (FR) › - Timepecker (IRE) › (Dansili (GB)) ›

b g Red Jazz (USA) › - Regal Ribbon (GB) › (Lawman (FR)) ›

b m Dragon Pulse (IRE) › - Weekend Getaway (IRE) › (Acclamation (GB)) ›

b g Cacique (IRE) › - Interim Payment (USA) › (Red Ransom (USA)) ›

b g Frankel (GB) › - Gilt Edge Girl (GB) › (Monsieur Bond (IRE)) ›

b g Showcasing (GB) › - Thousandkissesdeep (IRE) › (Night Shift (USA)) ›

b g Make Believe (GB) › - Manaka (FR) › (Falco (USA)) ›

b g Make Believe (GB) › - Malea (IRE) › (Oratorio (IRE)) ›

gr f Fast Company (IRE) › - Summer Dove (USA) › (Super Saver (USA)) ›

b g Awtaad (IRE) › - Zahoo (IRE) › (Nayef (USA)) ›

ch m Dragon Pulse (IRE) › - Blue Dune (GB) › (Invincible Spirit (IRE)) ›

13[11] ● Rockview Roman ›		7	9-0	J: Siobhan Rutledge ›[5]		47 72
64439- ♀ ⊟ ⊗ [1 tip] 144 (51J)			49	T: John C McConnell ›		
b g Holy Roman Emperor (IRE) › - Veneration (GB) › (Dalakhani (IRE)) ›						
14[3] ● Tooso › p		5	9-0	J: Chris Hayes ›		68 76
68060- ♀ ⊟ ⊗ 251			49	T: [1] S M Duffy ›		
b m Fast Company (IRE) › - Sulaalaat (GB) › (New Approach (IRE)) ›						
15[15] ● All Ways And Ever ›		4	8-12	J: James Ryan ›[7]		22 56
0/00-6 ♀ ⊟ ⊗ 12			47	T: T G McCourt ›		
b f Zoffany (IRE) › - Cloudy Miss (IRE) › (Shamardal (USA)) ›						
16[5] ● Starlight Rose ›		4	8-12	J: Gavin Ryan ›		39 73
00-**000** ♀ ⊟ ⊗ 62			47	T: Thomas Dowling ›		
ch f El Kabeir (USA) › - Twenty Roses (IRE) › (Mastercraftsman (IRE)) ›						
17[9] ● Tastyee › t		5	8-12	J: Wayne Lordan ›		63 75
00566- ♀ ⊟ ⊗ [1 tip] 174			47	T: David Kenneth Budds ›		
b m Markaz (IRE) › - Spirit Of Alsace (IRE) › (Invincible Spirit (IRE)) ›						
R18[16] ● Cleopatra's Needle › t		5	9-2	J: Ronan Whelan ›		49 72
7860-4 ♀ ⊟ ⊗ 20			51	T: H Rogers ›		
ch m Helmet (AUS) › - Philae (USA) › (Seeking The Gold (USA)) ›						
R19[20] ● Anycity › tb		7	9-7	J: Cian MacRedmond ›		- 70
6●06/5 ♀ ⊟ ⊗ 20			56	T: J Larkin ›		
b g Zoffany (IRE) › - Loquacity (GB) › (Diktat (GB)) ›						
R20[7] ● Ernest Loring › t		5	8-12	J:		- 69
0080/6 ♀ ⊟ ⊗ 13			47	T: J Larkin ›		
b g Red Jazz (USA) › - Sinegronto (IRE) › (Kheleyf (USA)) ›						

Our first race with two qualifiers by the same sire – horse number 1 Emperor Of Silk and horse number 13 Rockview Roman, both by Holy Roman Emperor

RESULT 5.45pm GOWRAN PARK

EMPEROR OF SILK 17TH 20/1 (BSP 36.0), AND ROCKVIEW ROMAN WON 15/2 (BSP 11.52)

Conclusions: I am writing this line before any of the horses above have run. I am not expecting any winners to be honest (*UPDATE – I AM SO PLEASED TO BE WRONG!), this is a long-term strategy where a betting bank seems the sensible option. There will and have been losing runs that need to be weathered, BUT the facts are there – historically you would have made decent, regular profits following these sires, and long may that continue! Our example day (by complete fluke I promise) gave us:

15 bets
5 winners

10 losers (so a 33% strike rate)

Points risked 15
Points returned 36.97
Profit on the day 21.97
Or 146.47% return on investment.

Of course this won't happen every day but hopefully you can now see how this can and does work.

Flat racing UK Turf by sire

Top 5 most profitable sires over the last 10 years

Sire	Runners	Winners	Strike Rate	Profit/Loss to BSP	Longest Winning Run	Longest Losing Run
Sixties Icon	2015	233	11.56%	+£1089.12	3	54
Bated Breath	2024	239	11.81%	+£799.24	3	47
Mount Nelson	1587	175	11.03%	+£758.73	2	44
Fountain Of Youth	447	43	9.62%	+£695.51	2	27
Dubawi	4087	822	20.11%	+£586.10	4	44

OK, well I won't be adding any notes after this and will leave you to draw your own conclusions but I will add that IF you had started with a big enough bank to ignore the long losing runs, then even at the most basic level (above) you would have made an after commission (and tax free) profit of over £39,000 to £10 stakes over the 10 years – we have found something here without any doubt so please, stick with it and read on!

Sixties Icon

Category		Runners	Winners	Strike Rate	Profit	LWR	LLR
Most profitable age	4	455	61	13.51%	+£1069.55	2	35
Most	Good	572	59	10.31%	+£885.13	2	53

Category		Runners	Winners	Strike Rate	Profit	LWR	LLR
profitable going							
Most profitable distance	6 furlongs	293	28	9.56%	+£940.63	3	48
Most profitable sex etc	Gelding	660	78	11.82%	+£964.12	2	38

Bated Breath

Category		Runners	Winners	Strike Rate	Profit	LWR	LLR
Most profitable age	3	773	92	11.90%	+£551.26	4	37
Most profitable going	Good	617	88	14.26%	+£442.38	3	24
Most profitable distance	6 furlongs	637	79	12.40%	+£823.72	4	37
Most profitable sex etc	Filly	786	99	12.60%	+£749.80	5	36

Mount Nelson

Category		Runners	Winners	Strike Rate	Profit	LWR	LLR
Most profitable age	3	576	73	12.67%	+£858.17	3	33
Most profitable going	Good to Firm	558	65	11.65%	+£789.89	3	26
Most profitable distance	1 mile	231	11	4.76%	+£710.53	1	65
Most profitable sex etc	Gelding	750	86	11.47%	+£847.83	2	38

Fountain Of Youth

Category		Runners	Winners	Strike Rate	Profit	LWR	LLR
Most profitable age	3	163	13	7.98%	+£683.77	2	40
Most profitable going	Good	161	18	11.18%	+£726.69	3	22
Most profitable distance	5 furlongs	141	10	7.09%	+£622.38	1	41
Most profitable sex etc	Gelding	229	23	10.04%	+£646.30	2	41

Dubawi

Category		Runners	Winners	Strike Rate	Profit	LWR	LLR
Most profitable age	3	1715	400	23.32%	+£542.20	5	27
Most profitable going	Good to Firm	1378	298	21.63%	+£387.27	4	31
Most profitable distance	10 furlongs	622	143	22.99%	+£197.04	5	39
Most profitable sex etc	Filly	1156	239	20.67%	+£488.96	4	46

Flat racing UK All-weather by sire

Top 5 most profitable sires over the last 10 years

Sire	Runners	Winners	Strike Rate	Profit/Loss to BSP	Longest Winning Run	Longest Losing Run

Dandy Man	2721	280	10.29%	+£687.24	3	53
Big Bad Bob	623	54	8.67%	+£470.58	1	37
Rail Link	596	75	12.58%	+£446.42	3	31
Exceed And Excel	4021	563	14.00%	+£423.66	4	53
Excellent Art	1024	109	10.64%	+£398.36	3	36

Dandy Man

Category		Runners	Winners	Strike Rate	Profit	LWR	LLR
Most profitable age	2	528	38	7.20%	+£521.34	2	36
Most profitable going	Standard	2721	280	10.29%	+£687.24	3	54
Most profitable distance	5 furlongs	627	70	11.16%	+£658.29	3	56
Most profitable sex etc	Gelding	1549	170	10.97%	+£943.00	3	50

Big Bad Bob

Category		Runners	Winners	Strike Rate	Profit	LWR	LLR
Most profitable age	2	116	7	6.03%	+£476.84	1	24
Most profitable going	Standard	623	54	8.67%	+£468.84	1	37
Most profitable distance	8 furlongs	185	14	757%	+£463.66	1	40
Most profitable	Filly	174	12	6.90%	+£456.01	1	33

sex etc						

Rail Link

Category		Runners	Winners	Strike Rate	Profit	LWR	LLR
Most profitable age	3	129	22	17.05%	+£205.45	2	29
Most profitable going	Standard	596	75	12.58%	+£446.42	3	31
Most profitable distance	12 furlongs	146	26	17.81%	+£235.14	2	31
Most profitable sex etc	Gelding	408	51	12.50%	+£246.03	3	37

Exceed And Excel

Category		Runners	Winners	Strike Rate	Profit	LWR	LLR
Most profitable age	2	530	92	17.36%	+£170.74	3	37
Most profitable going	Standard	4021	563	14.00%	+£423.66	4	53
Most profitable distance	8 furlongs	679	94	13.84%	+£127.77	4	32
Most profitable sex etc	Gelding	2495	330	13.23%	+£363.63	4	71

Excellent Art

Category		Runners	Winners	Strike Rate	Profit	LWR	LLR

Category		Runners	Winners	Strike Rate	Profit/Loss to BSP	Longest Winning Run	Longest Losing Run
Most profitable age	3	271	31	11.44%	+£382.92	2	34
Most profitable going	Standard	1024	109	10.64%	+£398.36	3	36
Most profitable distance	8 furlongs	259	29	11.20%	+£310.55	2	32
Most profitable sex etc	Gelding	602	66	10.96%	+£447.31	2	35

Flat racing Ireland Turf by sire

Top 5 most profitable sires over the last 10 years

Sire	Runners	Winners	Strike Rate	Profit/Loss to BSP	Longest Winning Run	Longest Losing Run
Sir Percy	200	13	6.50%	+£487.32	1	58
Captain Rio	462	50	10.82%	+£460.34	2	42
Starspangledbanner	527	59	11.20%	+£319.70	3	51
Holy Roman Emperor	1496	165	11.03%	+£306.00	3	50
Shamardal	829	87	10.49%	+£296.69	2	33

Sir Percy

Category		Runners	Winners	Strike Rate	Profit	LWR	LLR
Most profitable age	4	57	2	3.51%	+£275.63	1	29
Most profitable going	Soft	58	4	6.90%	+£299.57	1	28
Most profitable	10 furlongs	26	2	7.69%	+£319.15	1	17

distance							
Most profitable sex etc	Filly	59	7	11.86%	+£565.86	1	14

Captain Rio

Category		Runners	Winners	Strike Rate	Profit	LWR	LLR
Most profitable age	2	54	4	7.41%	+£143.57	1	27
Most profitable going	Good	169	16	9.47%	+£168.02	2	34
Most profitable distance	7 furlongs	133	16	12.03%	+£278.54	2	21
Most profitable sex etc	Colt	27	3	11.11%	+£239.38	1	17

Starspangledbanner

Category		Runners	Winners	Strike Rate	Profit	LWR	LLR
Most profitable age	2	211	31	14.69%	+£297.37	2	25
Most profitable going	Good	234	30	12.82%	+£208.56	2	30
Most profitable distance	6 furlongs	126	15	11.90%	+£251.91	1	17
Most profitable sex etc	Filly	290	34	11.72%	+£250.91	2	38

Holy Roman Emperor

Category		Runners	Winners	Strike Rate	Profit	LWR	LLR
Most profitable age	3	563	68	12.08%	+£206.22	4	58
Most profitable going	Good	609	71	11.66%	+£116.97	3	34
Most profitable distance	6 furlongs	209	22	10.53%	+£179.27	2	47
Most profitable sex etc	Filly	755	84	11.13%	+£191.72	3	30

Shamardal

Category		Runners	Winners	Strike Rate	Profit	LWR	LLR
Most profitable age	4	185	14	7.57%	+£197.00	1	42
Most profitable going	Good	357	34	9.52%	+£343.24	2	40
Most profitable distance	9 furlongs	42	4	9.52%	+£261.18	1	19
Most profitable sex etc	Filly	240	27	11.25%	+£339.45	3	22

Flat racing Ireland All-weather by sire

Top 5 most profitable sires over the last 10 years

Sire	Runners	Winners	Strike Rate	Profit/Loss to BSP	Longest Winning	Longest Losing

					Run	Run
Camacho	351	22	6.27%	+£482.56	2	41
Elzaam	301	33	10.96%	+£450.18	2	29
Lawman	378	27	7.14%	+£146.56	2	53
Verglas	179	28	15.64%	+£145.94	3	31
Vale Of York	105	11	10.48%	+£143.06	2	35

Camacho

Category		Runners	Winners	Strike Rate	Profit	LWR	LLR
Most profitable age	4	66	3	4.55%	+£284.21	1	43
Most profitable going	Standard	351	22	6.27%	+£482.56	1	41
Most profitable distance	7 furlongs	107	7	6.54%	+£498.05	1	25
Most profitable sex etc	Gelding	145	8	5.52%	+£308.14	1	37

Elzaam

Category		Runners	Winners	Strike Rate	Profit	LWR	LLR
Most profitable age	3	106	9	8.49%	+£439.88	1	23
Most profitable going	Standard	301	33	10.96%	+£450.18	2	28
Most profitable distance	10 furlongs	49	9	18.37%	+£359.69	2	17
Most profitable	Filly	97	5	5.15%	+£270.34	1	30

sex etc							

Lawman

Category		Runners	Winners	Strike Rate	Profit	LWR	LLR
Most profitable age	3	35	4	11.43%	+£100.06	2	20
Most profitable going	Standard	378	27	7.14%	+£146.56	2	53
Most profitable distance	7 furlongs	85	4	4.71%	+£189.95	1	42
Most profitable sex etc	Filly	130	11	8.46%	+£243.03	1	23

Verglas

Category		Runners	Winners	Strike Rate	Profit	LWR	LLR
Most profitable age	9	16	2	12.50%	+£53.19	1	13
Most profitable going	Standard	179	28	15.64%	+£145.94	3	31
Most profitable distance	6 furlongs	46	9	19.57%	+£96.07	2	9
Most profitable sex etc	Gelding	143	23	16.08%	+£131.22	3	24

Vale Of York

Category		Runners	Winners	Strike	Profit	LWR	LLR

				Rate			
Most profitable age	4	26	4	15.38%	+£141.22	2	11
Most profitable going	Standard	105	11	10.48%	+£143.06	2	35
Most profitable distance	7 furlongs	41	8	19.51%	+£181.04	2	13
Most profitable sex etc	Filly	48	5	10.42%	+£114.55	3	29

National Hunt racing UK (hurdles only) by sire

Top 5 most profitable sires over the last 10 years

Sire	Runners	Winners	Strike Rate	Profit/Loss to BSP	Longest Winning Run	Longest Losing Run
Echo Of Light	192	17	8.85%	+£747.07	3	28
No Risk At All	350	58	16.57%	+£523.20	3	35
Avonbridge	193	13	6.77%	+£416.68	2	38
Robin Des Champs	997	138	13.84%	+£415.78	3	43
Yeats	2380	331	13.91%	+£410.23	3	59

Echo Of Light

Category		Runners	Winners	Strike Rate	Profit	LWR	LLR
Most profitable age	5	51	6	11.76%	+£765.49	3	20
Most profitable going	Good	67	3	4.48%	+£514.81	2	46

Most profitable distance	16 furlongs	75	8	10.67%	+£775.99	2	17
Most profitable sex etc	Mare	42	6	14.29%	+£585.43	1	25

No Risk At All

Category		Runners	Winners	Strike Rate	Profit	LWR	LLR
Most profitable age	4	51	9	17.65%	+£522.79	2	14
Most profitable going	Good	114	24	21.05%	+£500.67	3	19
Most profitable distance	21 furlongs	25	4	16.00%	+£486.96	2	14
Most profitable sex etc	Filly	18	5	27.78%	+£526.45	2	5

Avonbridge

Category		Runners	Winners	Strike Rate	Profit	LWR	LLR
Most profitable age	4	21	4	19.05%	+£491.14	2	9
Most profitable going	Good to Soft	37	4	10.81%	+£484.33	1	12
Most profitable distance	17 furlongs	46	4	8.70%	+£433.06	1	19
Most profitable sex etc	Filly	15	1	6.67%	+£413.81	1	8

Robin Des Champs

Category		Runners	Winners	Strike Rate	Profit	LWR	LLR
Most profitable age	6	320	48	15.00%	+£163.68	6	33
Most profitable going	Good	330	58	17.58%	+£470.99	4	29
Most profitable distance	24 furlongs	74	8	10.81%	+£165.92	2	22
Most profitable sex etc	Gelding	721	106	14.70%	+£252.21	3	42

Yeats

Category		Runners	Winners	Strike Rate	Profit	LWR	LLR
Most profitable age	5	693	107	15.44%	+£342.04	3	29
Most profitable going	Good to Soft	620	81	13.06%	+£471.89	3	27
Most profitable distance	16 furlongs	376	46	12.23%	+£319.41	3	48
Most profitable sex etc	Mare	603	84	13.93%	+£411.28	3	44

National Hunt racing UK (Chases only) by sire

Top 5 most profitable sires over the last 10 years

Sire	Runners	Winners	Strike Rate	Profit/Loss to BSP	Longest Winning Run	Longest Losing Run
Lord America	112	15	13.39%	+£326.95	2	15
Whitmore's Conn	184	27	14.67%	+£294.61	2	24
King's Theatre	2530	398	15.73%	+£244.46	4	38
Midnight Legend	2349	377	16.05%	+£241.04	3	34
Alflora	1059	145	13.69%	+£240.38	3	30

Lord Americo

Category		Runners	Winners	Strike Rate	Profit	LWR	LLR
Most profitable age	10	20	5	20.00%	+£321.36	1	4
Most profitable going	Good	46	6	13.04%	+£298.65	1	13
Most profitable distance	33 furlongs	3	1	33.33%	+£296.89	1	2
Most profitable sex etc	Gelding	112	15	13.39%	+£326.95	2	15

Whitmore's Conn

Category		Runners	Winners	Strike Rate	Profit	LWR	LLR
Most profitable age	9	31	5	16.13%	+£332.06	2	10
Most profitable	Good to Soft	38	7	18.42%	+£326.34	2	15

going							
Most profitable distance	22	9	1	11.11%	+£308.94	1	5
Most profitable sex etc	Gelding	181	27	14.92%	+£297.61	2	21

King's Theatre

Category		Runners	Winners	Strike Rate	Profit	LWR	LLR
Most profitable age	10	291	45	15.46%	+£113.63	4	21
Most profitable going	Good	953	156	16.37%	+£219.85	3	25
Most profitable distance	24 furlongs	408	65	15.93%	+£191.42	2	23
Most profitable sex etc	Gelding	2261	338	14.95%	+£236.38	3	40

Midnight Legend

Category		Runners	Winners	Strike Rate	Profit	LWR	LLR
Most profitable age	15	3	1	33.33%	+£136.83	1	2
Most profitable going	Soft	588	89	15.14%	+£181.92	3	31
Most profitable distance	24 furlongs	297	44	14.81%	+£158.57	3	29
Most profitable sex etc	Gelding	1735	273	15.73%	+£174.18	3	48

Alflora

Category		Runners	Winners	Strike Rate	Profit	LWR	LLR
Most profitable age	11	126	17	13.49%	+£125.73	2	20
Most profitable going	Good	323	40	12.38%	+£108.42	3	41
Most profitable distance	28 furlongs	16	3	18.75%	+£64.76	2	5
Most profitable sex etc	Gelding	926	130	14.04%	+£236.23	3	26

National Hunt racing UK (bumpers only) by sire

Top 5 most profitable sires over the last 10 years

Sire	Runners	Winners	Strike Rate	Profit/Loss to BSP	Longest Winning Run	Longest Losing Run
Kayf Tara	1023	140	13.69%	+£384.90	4	42
Walk in The Park	191	32	16.75%	+£355.34	2	22
Shantou	306	48	15.69%	+£288.99	2	17
Presenting	720	108	15.00%	+£234.05	3	31
Gold Well	199	35	17.59%	+£133.69	2	13

Kayf Tara

Category		Runners	Winners	Strike Rate	Profit	LWR	LLR
Most profitable	6	158	14	8.86%	+£206.32	2	50

Category							
age							
Most profitable going	Good	366	47	12.84%	+£180.61	2	33
Most profitable distance	16 furlongs	659	90	13.66%	+£325.17	3	49
Most profitable sex etc	Gelding	481	77	16.01%	+£416.27	3	35

Walk In The Park

Category		Runners	Winners	Strike Rate	Profit	LWR	LLR
Most profitable age	4	88	12	13.64%	+£340.75	2	34
Most profitable going	Soft	52	6	11.54%	+£335.11	1	21
Most profitable distance	15 furlongs	54	8	14.81%	+£337.29	1	14
Most profitable sex etc	Filly	36	3	8.33%	+£333.20	1	25

Shantou

Category		Runners	Winners	Strike Rate	Profit	LWR	LLR
Most profitable age	7	8	1	12.50%	+£305.62	1	7
Most profitable going	Standard	18	2	11.11%	+£300.46	1	10
Most profitable distance	16 furlongs	199	31	15.58%	+£314.45	2	19

Most profitable sex etc	Gelding	229	41	17.90%	+£321.85	2	15

Presenting

Category		Runners	Winners	Strike Rate	Profit	LWR	LLR
Most profitable age	8	9	4	44.44%	+£146.64	2	2
Most profitable going	Standard	74	20	27.03%	+£278.34	2	9
Most profitable distance	16 furlongs	471	73	15.50%	+£152.38	2	32
Most profitable sex etc	Gelding	416	68	16.35%	+£207.75	3	21

Gold Well

Category		Runners	Winners	Strike Rate	Profit	LWR	LLR
Most profitable age	6	24	6	25.00%	+£111.78	3	8
Most profitable going	Good to Soft	41	8	19.51%	+£109.96	1	11
Most profitable distance	16 furlongs	133	23	17.29%	+£124.98	2	15
Most profitable sex etc	Mare	45	11	24.44%	+£150.57	3	10

National Hunt racing Ireland (hurdles only) by sire

Top 5 most profitable sires over the last 10 years

Sire	Runners	Winners	Strike Rate	Profit/Loss to BSP	Longest Winning Run	Longest Losing Run
Oscar	2541	228	8.97%	+£1164.90	3	64
Vertical Speed	116	6	5.17%	+£1026.04	2	29
Dushyantor	224	12	5.36%	+£990.45	2	33
Famous Name	232	13	5.60%	+£785.26	2	53
Zoffany	315	21	6.67%	+£761.04	2	47

<u>Oscar</u>

Category		Runners	Winners	Strike Rate	Profit	LWR	LLR
Most profitable age	4	108	11	10.19%	+£927.83	2	21
Most profitable going	Soft	912	89	9.76%	+£1017.97	3	85
Most profitable distance	16 furlongs	825	73	8.85%	+£620.30	2	37
Most profitable sex etc	Gelding	1463	147	10.05%	+£911.32	3	43

<u>Vertical Speed</u>

Category		Runners	Winners	Strike Rate	Profit	LWR	LLR
Most profitable age	6	35	1	2.86%	+£945.02	1	26
Most	Heavy	16	1	6.25%	+£964.02	1	12

Category		Runners	Winners	Strike Rate	Profit	LWR	LLR
profitable going							
Most profitable distance	16 furlongs	50	3	6.00%	+£1057.45	1	25
Most profitable sex etc	Mare	30	1	3.33%	+£950.02	1	21

Dushyantor

Category		Runners	Winners	Strike Rate	Profit	LWR	LLR
Most profitable age	8	41	4	9.76%	+£984.70	2	27
Most profitable going	Soft	74	4	5.41%	+£965.52	1	26
Most profitable distance	20	54	5	9.26%	+£1027.17	1	17
Most profitable sex etc	Gelding	174	10	5.75%	+£962.93	2	304

Famous Name

Category		Runners	Winners	Strike Rate	Profit	LWR	LLR
Most profitable age	4	58	1	1.72%	+£787.64	1	53
Most profitable going	Good	110	8	7.27%	+£809.86	2	48
Most profitable distance	16 furlongs	105	4	3.81%	+£797.33	1	39
Most profitable	Gelding	166	8	4.82%	+£748.33	1	77

sex etc							

Zoffany

Category		Runners	Winners	Strike Rate	Profit	LWR	LLR
Most profitable age	4	135	9	6.67%	+£871.08	1	31
Most profitable going	Good	140	12	8.57%	+£894.93	1	26
Most profitable distance	16 furlongs	213	14	6.57%	+£827.99	2	47
Most profitable sex etc	Gelding	240	18	7.50%	+£813.10	2	42

National Hunt racing Ireland (chases only) by sire

Top 5 most profitable sires over the last 10 years

Sire	Runners	Winners	Strike Rate	Profit/Loss to BSP	Longest Winning Run	Longest Losing Run
Court Cave	666	55	8.26%	+£555.58	2	34
Windsor Knot	117	11	9.40%	+£294.09	1	41
Yeats	581	78	13.43%	+£288.80	3	24
Witness Box	313	23	7.35%	+£218.07	2	35
Kayf Tara	439	51	11.62%	+£170.00	2	49

Court Cave

Category		Runners	Winners	Strike	Profit	LWR	LLR

				Rate			
Most profitable age	9	78	4	5.13%	+£320.80	2	32
Most profitable going	Good	312	31	9.94%	+£396.68	2	26
Most profitable distance	17 furlongs	63	7	11.11%	+£347.67	2	27
Most profitable sex etc	Gelding	462	36	7.79%	+£405.68	3	80

Windsor Knot

Category		Runners	Winners	Strike Rate	Profit	LWR	LLR
Most profitable age	5	14	1	7.14%	+£266.56	1	12
Most profitable going	Good	62	9	14.52%	+£310.47	1	19
Most profitable distance	19 furlongs	13	3	23.08%	+£286.12	1	5
Most profitable sex etc	Mare	10	1	10.00%	+£270.56	1	8

Yeats

Category		Runners	Winners	Strike Rate	Profit	LWR	LLR
Most profitable age	5	41	6	14.63%	+£158.69	1	10
Most profitable going	Good to Soft	109	19	17.43%	+£138.29	2	15

Most profitable distance	19 furlongs	54	4	7.41%	+£130.27	2	32
Most profitable sex etc	Gelding	306	45	14.71%	+£309.25	4	42

Witness Box

Category		Runners	Winners	Strike Rate	Profit	LWR	LLR
Most profitable age	9	49	3	6.12%	+£140.03	1	18
Most profitable going	Good to Soft	23	4	17.39%	+£195.92	1	9
Most profitable distance	22 furlongs	37	2	5.41%	+£152.92	1	14
Most profitable sex etc	Gelding	281	22	7.83%	+£243.76	2	34

Kayf Tara

Category		Runners	Winners	Strike Rate	Profit	LWR	LLR
Most profitable age	9	50	6	12.00%	+£219.11	1	14
Most profitable going	Soft	153	19	12.42%	+£143.83	2	23
Most profitable distance	20 furlongs	87	10	11.49%	+£153.23	1	21
Most profitable sex etc	Mare	68	7	10.29%	+£158.26	2	19

National Hunt racing Ireland (bumpers only) by sire

Top 5 most profitable sires over the last 10 years

Sire	Runners	Winners	Strike Rate	Profit/Loss to BSP	Longest Winning Run	Longest Losing Run
Califet	113	6	5.31%	+£895.29	1	30
Mountain High	144	15	10.42%	+£468.15	1	24
Court Cave	242	19	7.85%	+£370.95	2	42
King's Theatre	323	56	17.34%	+£212.35	4	21
Mahler	336	36	10.71%	+£197.09	2	32

Califet

Category		Runners	Winners	Strike Rate	Profit	LWR	LLR
Most profitable age	5	59	4	6.78%	+£935.99	1	25
Most profitable going	Soft	43	1	2.33%	+£937.02	1	30
Most profitable distance	16 furlongs	77	6	7.79%	+£931.29	1	25
Most profitable sex etc	Mare	34	3	8.82%	+£957.96	1	144

Mountain High

Category		Runners	Winners	Strike Rate	Profit	LWR	LLR

Most profitable age	4	43	8	18.60%	+£406.83	3	12
Most profitable going	Good	76	11	14.47%	+£512.90	2	20
Most profitable distance	16 furlongs	92	9	9.78%	+£339.02	1	28
Most profitable sex etc	Filly	14	3	21.43%	+£380.30	2	85

Court Cave

Category		Runners	Winners	Strike Rate	Profit	LWR	LLR
Most profitable age	5	110	10	9.09%	+£327.95	2	43
Most profitable going	Heavy	34	1	2.94%	+£278.61	1	20
Most profitable distance	20 furlongs	18	1	5.56%	+£294.61	1	14
Most profitable sex etc	Gelding	136	11	8.09%	+£343.56	2	33

King's Theatre

Category		Runners	Winners	Strike Rate	Profit	LWR	LLR
Most profitable age	5	162	32	19.75%	+£279.33	3	16
Most profitable going	Good to Firm	27	6	22.22%	+£216.09	1	8
Most	16	217	37	17.05%	+£186.46	3	17

Category						
profitable distance	furlongs					
Most profitable sex etc	Mare	181	30	16.57%	+£254.14	2	24

Mahler

Category		Runners	Winners	Strike Rate	Profit	LWR	LLR
Most profitable age	5	136	18	13.24%	+£183.63	3	24
Most profitable going	Good to Soft	43	7	16.28%	+£204.28	1	13
Most profitable distance	20 furlongs	17	1	5.88%	+£146.45	1	12
Most profitable sex etc	Mare	108	11	10.19%	+£137.69	3	32

Gambling Harm

As I write the Gambling review is coming, and centre stage in many people's minds – but that is a discussion for elsewhere. This book is not meant to encourage anyone to gamble, and I urge you all to think twice before placing any bets to make sure you can afford your hobby. For me, racing is exciting and fun – it's not about the gambling, it's about pitting my wits against those who compile the odds – and trying to find a way to beat the bookmakers – I can do that with small **affordable** bets and suggest you do the same. Do NOT let gambling overcome you, do NOT bet more than you can afford to lose – and DO make the most of all the tools available with your bookmaker such as time outs and deposit limits if needed. Please please control your gambling (do not let it control you) and remember that help is available via the National Gambling Helpline (0808 8020 133), and online at Gamcare.org.uk with other services freely available.

Testimonials:

"Sean and I have worked together for many years now, and his knowledge of racing is well known and respected throughout the industry. If the articles and opinion shared with readers of News - The World of Sport are any indication as to just how valuable this book will be to punters, then it's a "must have" weapon in your punting arsenal. If you do not bet using stats, you will lose more often than you win and, whether you bet for profit or fun, you need this on your side"

Ron Robinson – Owner, The World of Sport

"Sean Trivass is better known as the 'Statman' to my readers and has contributed excellent comprehensive articles on horse racing for my monthly newsletter What really Wins Money. His stats angles are totally unique and a real deep dive into the world of horse racing stats based betting angles.

He's looked at jockeys, trainers, race courses, sires and dams (breeding), the draw, the all weather, favourites, 2nd and 3rd favourites , ground conditions, race distance, handicaps versus non-handicap and many other angles, for both the horse racing backer and layer.

There have been some real eye-catching finds from Sean's work, some of which I use myself. This guy knows his onions! "

Clive Keeling – What Really Wins Money

"Statistics can be presented in many a varied manner for varied reasons and we are right to retain a sceptical mind of them and how and why they are revealed. However, with horse racing they are a vital component and my colleague Sean Trivass is an equally vital component in collating and interpreting them for our use.

Watching, listening, reading Sean's dissection of a field using his calibrated statistics is a racing marvel. He professes to not liking full-sized handicap fields, but in reality he is in his element pouring over the variables using his statistics as he slices and dices the field into a logical order for the likes of you and I to understand.

Group 1 elite contests to the full field handicaps are all part of Sean's vision and depth of years of experience. From watching the world's best on the track to a humble maiden, he approaches each contest with the same enthusiasm to find the outcome

I have watched and enjoyed Sean's work for twenty years as we have travelled to race meetings in many parts of the globe and when back home in Australia he is my guide for UK racing. Racing is international, broadcasting 24 hours a day somewhere in the world, and Sean's delving into the statistics give us all a steady platform to participate".

Rob Burnet
Editor
Thoroughbrednews.com.au

Finally, should you have any questions (no abuse thank you, all of this has been written in good faith) or just want to know a little bit more about my upcoming projects and books, feel free to contact me via www.writesports.net

©Sean Trivass 2023

Printed in Great Britain
by Amazon

40422978R00033